"There are few things that elementary-aged kids love more than amazing facts. The Good Book Company's *All About...* series presents fabulous facts alongside astounding photos and engaging Bible history in a kid-friendly package that will inspire children to crave God's word!"

Danika Cooley, Author, Bible Road Trip™ (ThinkingKidsPress.com) and *Help Your Kids Learn and Love the Bible*

"*All About Bible Animals* is a very clever book! Yes, it's filled with fun facts about the animals found in the Bible. But it introduces those animals chronologically, unpacking the story of the Bible as it goes along. So the reader learns about wonderful animals while, at the same time, discovering the wonders of God's love."

Bob Hartman, Author, *The Prisoners, the Earthquake, and the Midnight Song*

"Anyone acquainted with young children knows that 'why' is one of those first words asked multiple times daily. That curiosity doesn't end as we mature, since the Lord gave us inquisitive minds. His astounding creation fascinates us as we seek to peel back the layers and understand with our finite minds a hint of the genius found in every single thing he created. The glorious variety seen in the animal kingdom alone points us to the creativity of our great God. *All About Bible Animals* illustrates this point so well and is such a fun read for kids of all ages. The tidbits of lesser-known details involving carefully selected Bible animals and the settings in which they are encountered in Scripture, coupled with the beautiful photography and graphics, cause us to marvel, laugh and yearn to know more. My growing library for my grandchildren will be greatly enhanced by what is another winner from this series. I highly recommend it!"

Mary Mohler, President's Wife, Southern Seminary; Director, Seminary Wives Institute; Author, *Growing in Gratitude*

ALL ABOUT...

BIBLE ANIMALS

**Over 100 amazing facts about
the animals of the Bible**

Written by | Design by
Simona Piscioneri | **André Parker**

thegoodbook
COMPANY

ALL ABOUT BIBLE ANIMALS

Animals are such an important part of our world, from the smallest of insects to the largest of the animal kingdom. But which ones were important in the Bible, and why? Were animals viewed the same way thousands of years ago as they are today?

This book starts with the very first animals that God created. Each double-page spread introduces another incredible creature, with fascinating facts, Bible quotes and picture references. Tricky Bible words and concepts are explained throughout, as we discover which Bible animals were valued, feared, disliked, or even part of a miraculous rescue!

As we journey through the Bible, we'll find out that God can even use animals to help fulfil his plans and promises (and he often does).

All About: Bible Animals | © The Good Book Company 2023

thegoodbook.com | thegoodbook.co.uk | thegoodbook.com.au | thegoodbook.co.nz | thegoodbook.co.in

Unless indicated, all Scripture references are taken from the Holy Bible, New International Reader's Version. Copyright © 2014 Biblica, Inc. Used by permission.

QUIZ ANSWERS (page 46)

1. c. The Bible doesn't tell us. (p 8) | 2. a (p 15) | 3. c. (p 16-17) | 4. b. (p 20-21) | 5. c. (p 23) | 6. c. (p 26) | 7. b and c. (p 40-41) | 8. c (p 44)

Written by Simona Piscioneri | Design by André Parker | All photos licensed from iStock.com

ISBN: 9781784988685 | Printed in India

Contents

The first animals	4
A very sneaky snake	6
The dove that got away	8
Flocks and herds	10
Frog overload!	12
A land of bees and honey	14
Bravery vs bear	16
The thirsty deer	18
Raven delivery-service	20
Lions on a diet	22
How big was that fish?	24
The sheep who found out first	26
Locusts for lunch	28
A very fishy miracle	30
God looks after sparrows	32
Remember to feed the dog!	34
In the pigpen	36
The overloaded camel	38
A king on a donkey	40
When a rooster's crow makes you cry	42
Everyone is welcome	44
Quiz time	46
Glossary	47

THE FIRST ANIMALS

Leopard

A nimals appear in the first chapter of the Bible. God made all kinds of animals even before he made people.

Genesis chapter 1 tells us that God created the universe and **EVERYTHING** in it with his power. He spoke light into existence, and mountains and trees and oceans, and habitats for all kinds of creatures. God invented feathers and fins, fur and fangs, and he did it in six days!

EVERYTHING?!

Orangutan

Leafcutter ants

We don't know exactly which year "the beginning" was, but we do know that God was there.

Genesis chapter 1 verse 1

In the beginning, God created the heavens and the earth.

Green tree frog

Garden snail

The biggest superpower

It's thought there are about 8.7 million different animal species in the world, though only 2.1 million have been found and named so far. Can you imagine inventing millions of animals? Just because humans could never do this, it doesn't mean God couldn't. God really is that powerful!

*The aye-aye is a long-fingered lemur found only in Madagascar. It is the world's largest nocturnal primate.

Clown fish

Craziest creatures

What's the weirdest animal you've ever heard of? The aye-aye*, platypus, sloth, axolotl or blobfish? These are just some of the unique creatures (who don't get a mention in the Bible) that show us the vastness of God's imagination!

Axolotl

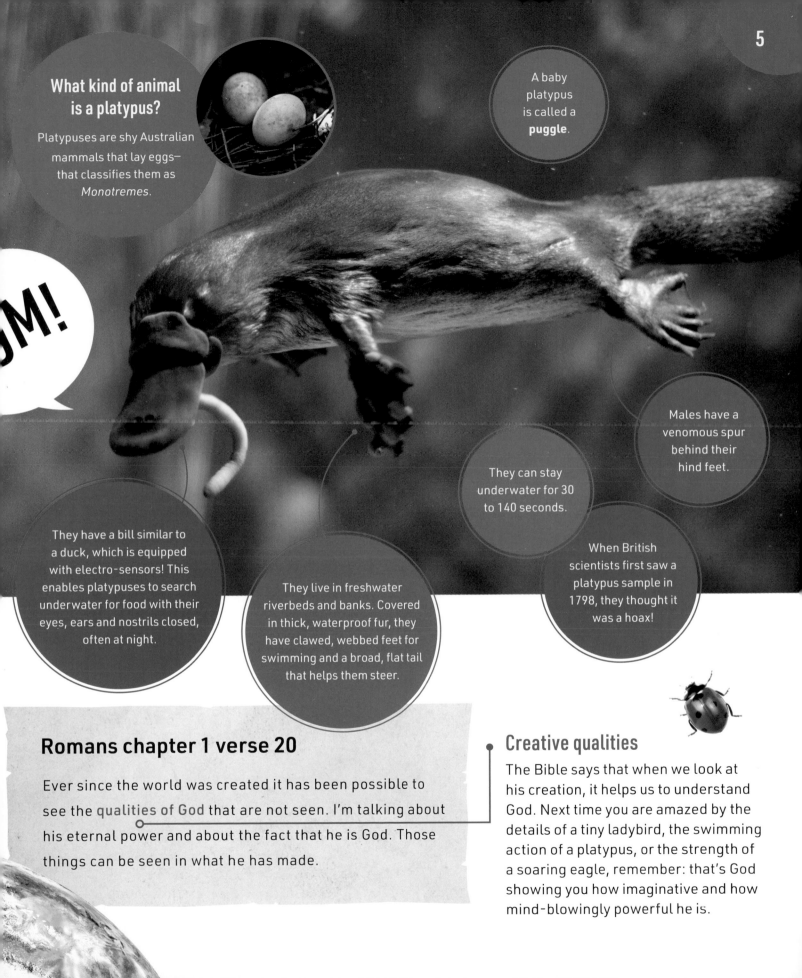

What kind of animal is a platypus?

Platypuses are shy Australian mammals that lay eggs— that classifies them as *Monotremes*.

A baby platypus is called a **puggle**.

JM!

Males have a venomous spur behind their hind feet.

They can stay underwater for 30 to 140 seconds.

They have a bill similar to a duck, which is equipped with electro-sensors! This enables platypuses to search underwater for food with their eyes, ears and nostrils closed, often at night.

They live in freshwater riverbeds and banks. Covered in thick, waterproof fur, they have clawed, webbed feet for swimming and a broad, flat tail that helps them steer.

When British scientists first saw a platypus sample in 1798, they thought it was a hoax!

Romans chapter 1 verse 20

Ever since the world was created it has been possible to see the qualities of God that are not seen. I'm talking about his eternal power and about the fact that he is God. Those things can be seen in what he has made.

Creative qualities

The Bible says that when we look at his creation, it helps us to understand God. Next time you are amazed by the details of a tiny ladybird, the swimming action of a platypus, or the strength of a soaring eagle, remember: that's God showing you how imaginative and how mind-blowingly powerful he is.

A VERY SNEAKY SNAKE

Proceed with caution!

Slithering, scaly and potentially scary, snakes often make people feel uncomfortable. But the Bible tells us about a talking snake! It's in Genesis chapter 3, not long after God finished his perfect creation.

Snakes rely on external heat sources to warm them up; that's why they're called "cold-blooded".

Egyptian cobra

Genesis chapter 3 verses 1-4

¹ The serpent said to the woman, "Did God really say, 'You must not eat fruit from any tree in the garden'?"

² The woman said to the serpent, "We may eat fruit from the trees in the garden. ³ But God did say, 'You must not eat the fruit from the tree in the middle of the garden. Do not even touch it. If you do, you will die.'"

⁴ "You will certainly not die," the serpent said.

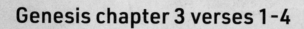

Snake facts
There are more than 3,000 snake species in the world, with 20% being venomous.

Children's python

Tree python

Who was really talking?
While snakes can be dangerous, they are not evil. The serpent in this story was really God's enemy, Satan, who lied to Adam and Eve in order to convince them not to trust God.

Some snakes can be kept as pets. Someone who loves snakes is called an ophiophilist.

Corn snakes

Most snakes lay eggs, while those in cold climates often give birth to live young.

Snakes don't have eyelids or good eyesight. They smell with their flickering tongue.

Reticulated pythons are the longest snakes. In 1912 one was measured at 10 metres (33 feet) long!

Blue pit viper

Serpent or snake?

In the original language that Genesis was written in, "serpent" and "snake" are the same word. Some people think that because God cursed serpents to crawl on their belly (Genesis 3 v 14), they may have previously had legs like other reptiles.

Warning flags!

1. There is a talking snake in this story.
2. Actions have consequences.
3. The snake said God's rules couldn't be trusted.
4. Adam and Eve believed the snake instead of trusting God—and ate the fruit. (Oh no!)

Curses and consequences

When Adam and Eve ate the fruit they weren't supposed to eat, it started a chain reaction of bad things including fear, shame, pain and even death. Their perfect friendship with God was broken, and they had to leave God's perfect garden.

But God made Adam and Eve a promise. He would make a way for his perfect friendship with people to be restored (see page 43).

THE DOVE THAT GOT AWAY

When Noah was alive, sin and meanness and hurt were everywhere! But God noticed Noah doing what was right, so he made a rescue plan to save Noah's family and two of every animal from the consequences of other people's sin. In Genesis chapter 6, God told Noah to build a gigantic, box-like boat he called an ark, to stay safe from a flood that was going to destroy the earth.

Dove facts
A white dove is a symbol of peace or love. The Bible doesn't tell us what coloured dove Noah released from the ark.

Pigeons and doves produce a "milk" from their glands to feed their young. They are the only birds who do this.

Turtle dove

How big?
God gave Noah the exact size to build the ark. It was...

- longer than a football or soccer field.
- higher than a modern four-storey house.
- long and skinny in shape, being ten times longer than it was wide.
- built with a similar storage capacity as about 450 trucks!

Some people have built modern-day versions of Noah's ark, to show how big it was.

Doves, along with about 90% of all birds, keep the same partner over their lifetime.

Doves are strong fliers, have an excellent sense of direction and can find their way home from a long distance away.

Doves and pigeons are from the same bird family.

The ultimate lockdown!

Once the ark was finished and Noah's family and the animals were all inside, it started to rain. It rained NON-STOP for 40 days and nights. That's one long, noisy, smelly lockdown!

Genesis chapter 7 verses 14-15

[14] Noah ...had every kind of livestock, creature that moves along the ground, and bird that flies. [15] Pairs of all living creatures that breathe came to Noah and entered the ark.

Land - ho!

When the rain stopped, the earth was still flooded. How would Noah know when the water levels were low enough for everyone to safely leave the ark? There was one animal whose flying ability and natural instinct to find its way back home would prove very helpful.

Noah sent out a dove once a week, knowing it would come back to the ark if there was nowhere to land. On the 3rd week, the dove didn't return, and Noah knew it had found somewhere to make a new home. So a dove was the first animal to get out of ark-lockdown.

What's that word: Sin

Sometimes sin is easy to see, like people doing bad things in the story of Noah. Really though, sin is doing what *we* want instead of what *God* wants. It's not accepting that God is in charge and that his way is best. The first sin in the Bible was when Adam and Eve disobeyed God's one rule in the garden (see page 7).

1. Pink-headed fruit dove
2. Jambu fruit dove
3. Nicobar pigeon

FLOCKS AND HERDS

W ere there farmers in the Bible? Absolutely. But farming was a bit different in Bible times!

Which animals?

Sheep, goats, donkeys, cows and camels were farmed in groups called flocks or herds.

What was a farm like?

Abraham was one of the first farmers in the Bible. God chose him to be the father of a family that would become a great nation (the Israelites). While he was waiting for the homeland God had promised, Abraham and his family lived in tents and moved whenever needed to find shelter, food and water for their flocks and herds. Herd animals prefer to stick together—making it easier to move large numbers of animals from place to place.

Sheep grazing on the Mount of Olives. Israel

A sign of wealth

Genesis 24 v 1 says, "The LORD had blessed Abraham in every way". Having lots of animals was a sign of wealth, showing that you had plenty of everything, including milk and cheese, meat, wool, leather from animal skins, and transport for people and goods.

Later in the Bible, when Jesus was born (see page 27), most people lived in cities and towns, and being a shepherd was seen as a smelly, grubby, unimportant job.

Goaty facts

Unlike sheep, who graze on grass, goats eat a variety of foods including leaves, hay, grains and bark. Although they may nibble at anything (like clothes), that is a goat's way of exploring whether something is edible.

Because goats are flock animals, they can get lonely or depressed if they are kept alone.

Many goat species originate in mountain areas, so they love to climb. Sometimes they even climb into trees!

BaAa

Baby goats are called kids and are renowned for crazy jumping and bouncing.

The tricky issue of animal sacrifice

In the Bible, people offered animal sacrifices to honour God, to thank him and to say sorry for the mistakes they had made. The animals that died were usually sheep or goats, but sometimes cows or some birds were used. This might sound like a terrible thing to do if you are an animal lover! But when people offered an animal to God as a sacrifice, they were saying, "I'm giving something valuable to God".

Spots and speckles

In Genesis 30 v 31-43, Abraham's grandson Jacob took all the spotted and speckled goats and sheep from a combined herd as payment for his work. Most sheep in Bible times were white, and most goats were black or brown. Not many of either animal were patterned. In a very unusual breeding programme, God blessed Jacob, and he ended up with lots of healthy spotty lambs and speckly kids.

FROG OVERLOAD!

If you like amphibians, this story is for you! While God's people, the Israelites, were waiting for a homeland of their own, they found themselves in slavery in Egypt, under a mean king called Pharaoh. God heard his people's cries for freedom, so he used a guy called Moses, some nasty diseases, and a whole heap of frogs, to carry out an amazing rescue plan.

Frog facts

Frogs are amphibians—they can live in water or on land but need both. They don't drink water; they absorb it through their skin.

Frogs' hind legs are more than twice as long as their front ones. So they can leap 20 times their own body length!

Common frog

Yellow-banded poison dart frog

Ten plagues

Water turned to blood
Frogs
Gnats (lice)
Flies
Sickness of livestock
Boils (pus-filled sores)
Hail
Locusts
Darkness
Death of the firstborn

Epic power struggle

Pharaoh didn't want the Israelites to go free—they were his slaves! He also didn't want to admit that anyone was more powerful than him. So when Moses said, "The LORD is the God of Israel. He says, 'Let my people go'" (Exodus 5 v 1), Pharaoh said, *NO!*

God sent ten revolting **plagues** before Pharaoh changed his mind.

Uh oh!

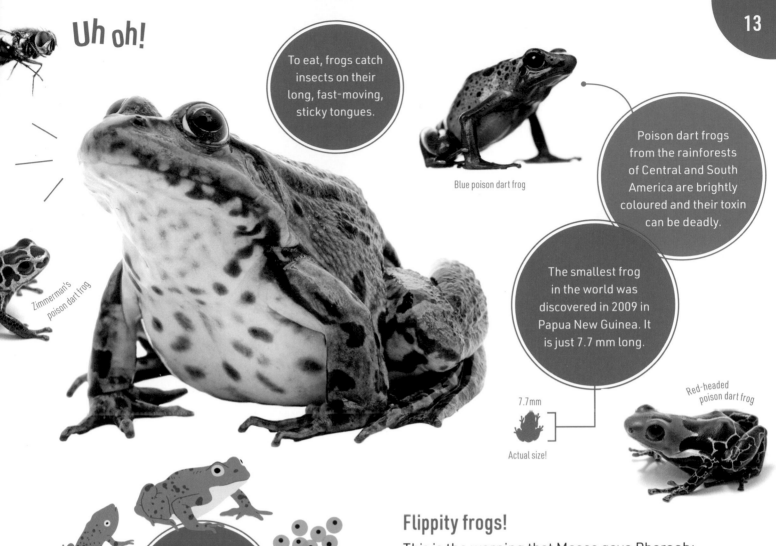

To eat, frogs catch insects on their long, fast-moving, sticky tongues.

Blue poison dart frog

Poison dart frogs from the rainforests of Central and South America are brightly coloured and their toxin can be deadly.

The smallest frog in the world was discovered in 2009 in Papua New Guinea. It is just 7.7 mm long.

7.7mm

Actual size!

Zimmerman's poison dart frog

Red-headed poison dart frog

A frog's life-cycle progresses from an egg to a tadpole to a frog through a process of metamorphosis.

Flippity frogs!

This is the warning that Moses gave Pharaoh: "The Nile River will be full of frogs. They will come up into your palace. You will have frogs in your bedroom and on your bed. They will be in the homes of your officials and your people. They will be in your ovens and in the bowls for kneading your bread. The frogs will be on you, your people and all your officials." (Exodus 8 v 3-4) That sounds very slimy!

Pick your plague

Which do you think is worse: frogs in your bedroom, lice all over your body or locusts that eat all the crops? None of them sound very good! Sadly, it wasn't until the last plague when his own son died, that Pharaoh finally admitted that God was in charge and let the Israelites go free.

God protected his people from that final plague. The night of the rescue, called Passover, is still celebrated by Jewish people over 3,000 years later.

What's that word: Plague

An unusually large infestation of insects, animals or disease that causes severe damage.

A LAND OF BEES AND HONEY

Have you heard of these nicknames for places?

The Emerald Isle (Ireland)

The Big Apple (New York)

The Land Down Under (Australia)

The City of Light (Paris)

How about the "Land of Plenty of Milk and Honey"? It sounds like something from a fairytale, but that's how God described the homeland he promised to his people the Israelites. And where there's honey, there are bees!

Did you know?

Bees are amazing architects! They create perfectly formed hexagons out of beeswax within their hives. This is called honeycomb, and is where the honey is stored, and where bee-eggs are laid.

What's in a name?

When God promised a land of "plenty of *milk and honey*" did he mean there was so much honey that it was oozing out of the ground?

No, but having plenty of *honey* means lots of fruit trees and flowers for bees to find nectar and pollen.

To have plenty of *milk*, the land would have food, fresh water, shelter and shade for goats and cows.

God was promising a land that was full of good things; a land that overflowed with more than what was needed. God wanted his people to have a wonderful place to live.

Bees have five eyes and six legs.

Only the honeybee species makes honey from nectar and pollen. About 5% of bee species are honeybees.

Archaeologists have found the remains of a 3,000-year-old man-made beehive in Israel.

In nature, bees nest in trees, rock-crevices or in the ground.

The buzz on bees

Bees collect nectar and pollen from plants on their legs. This helps plants to produce fruit, vegetables and seeds, because bees transfer pollen from one plant to another in a process called pollination.

Most bees live in large colonies, with thousands of bees working together. The queen bee, worker bees and drones all have specific roles in the bee colony.

Bee populations are getting smaller around the world.

The long way around

The story of the Israelites entering the promised land ends up being the longest camping trip in history! Sadly, God's people weren't very good at trusting God's promises, so they had to wait 40 years to get there! (Find out what happened in a book of the Bible called Numbers, chapters 13 and 14.)

God had promised a homeland filled with good things, but because his people didn't trust him they were stuck in a dry, barren desert. Don't worry though, God kept his promise 40 years later, when the next generation entered the land of Israel instead. I wonder if honey was one of the first things they ate when they got there?

BRAVERY vs BEAR

Were there any dangerous animals in Israel in Bible times? If you count lions, venomous snakes, scorpions, wolves and bears, the answer is yes!

The only bear species from this part of the world—the Syrian brown bear—no longer lives in Israel, but they were once a real threat to both people and livestock.

Would you argue with a bear?

The Bible tells us about a teenager named David, who looked after his father's sheep. His older brothers had more important jobs (like fighting in the army), but David used his time as a shepherd to protect the flock. He wasn't going to let a bear run off with one of his sheep!

1 Samuel chapter 17 verses 34-35

David said ... "Sometimes a lion or a bear would come and carry off a sheep from the flock. Then I would go after it and hit it. I would save the sheep it was carrying in its mouth."

FYI If you live somewhere close to bears, chasing them is not recommended!

Syrian brown bears

Syrian brown bears are the smallest species of brown bear— but at 2 metres (6.5 feet) high when standing on their hind legs, and weighing about twice as much as an average man, they are not that small!

Syrian brown bears are the only bears to have white claws. Their fur is light brown.

David killed Goliath with a stone from his shepherd's sling.

Training ground

David is more well-known for fighting a bigger, ruder, more dangerous opponent than a bear. A gigantic man called Goliath, from Israel's enemies the Philistines, had the whole army terrified. None of the soldiers wanted to face him. It took the young shepherd David, who had practised on lions and bears, to challenge Goliath and bring him down.

The bigger hero

Was it really David who defeated Goliath though? Was it his bravery that beat the bears? Even David himself didn't think that. He said:

1 Samuel chapter 17 verse 37

"The LORD saved me from the paw of the lion. He saved me from the paw of the bear. And he'll save me from the powerful hand of this Philistine too."

Brown bears do not stay in family groups. Cubs are raised by their mums.

Bear-y important information

Brown bears are omnivorous, meaning they eat both meat (grubs, fish, rodents and small mammals) and plants (nuts, seeds, berries, fruit and grains). They also love honey.

Brown 'Grizzly' bear

GrRRRR

Although males are usually territorial, mama bears become very aggressive when protecting their cubs.

Their life span is 20 – 25 years in the wild.

Eventually, the brave shepherd boy David became king of Israel, and he continued to trust that God is more powerful than any animal, person or situation he could ever face.

THE THIRSTY DEER

S hhhhh!!!
Have you ever unexpectedly come across an animal in the wild? Perhaps you started moving very slowly, trying not to startle it, hoping you might get close enough to take a photo (or far enough away to be safe!).

If you are keen on spotting deer, here's a tip: deer will probably see, smell and hear you a long time before you find them.

Poetry in motion

Deer are majestic creatures. In the Bible, mighty warrior King David (who was also a musician and a poet), mentioned deer in some of his poems. Once when he was feeling sad and forgotten he said:

Psalm 42 verses 1-2

[1] A deer longs for streams of water. God, I long for you in the same way. [2] I am thirsty for God.

Male deer, called bucks or stags, have antlers, which they shed in winter. They grow new ones each spring.

Fallow deer stag

The two main species of deer in Israel were the Persian fallow and the smaller roe deer.

Roe deer fawn

That's an unusual thing to say, partly because most of the water that deer need comes from the plants they eat. They still need some water to drink, but if a deer was really thirsty, it would either be because it had just been chased by a predator or because it didn't have enough fresh, juicy shrubs to eat.

Thirst-quencher

David was in a tough situation, like the thirsty deer. He needed the life-giving love of God to satisfy his dry and thirsty emotions. Sometimes when we feel sad and forgotten, we don't know what we need. Try doing what David did and reach out to God for help.

Deer details

Deer are shy animals, and highly alert to possible danger from many predators who consider them a tasty meal.

Deer can move their ears independently of each other, to catch sounds from different directions.

Deer are herbivores, and will snack on almost any kind of plant.

Their sense of smell is about 1,000 times stronger than a human's!

Other strengths include speed, sure-footed climbing, leaping, swimming and the instinct to camouflage and freeze.

Persian fallow deer

Still thirsty?

Jesus once offered a woman he met "living water", saying that if she had it, she would never be thirsty again. That sounds pretty good! Jesus, like David, was saying that really getting to know God can satisfy us on the inside, where we are hungry and thirsty for God's love. (Read that story in John chapter 4.)

RAVEN DELIVERY-SERVICE

A group of ravens is called an *unkindness* of ravens. Someone must have had a bad experience to give them that name! Perhaps they didn't know the Bible story about ravens saving a man's life by delivering food to him in a drought. That sounds like a very kind thing to do!

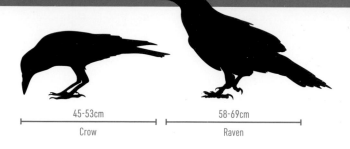

45-53cm
Crow

58-69cm
Raven

Are ravens good or bad?

Some people used to think that seeing lots of big, black ravens or crows flying together meant something bad was about to happen. That definitely wasn't Elijah's experience!

Elijah was a prophet who followed God. He told the king of Israel that there would be a long drought—a time where there would be no rain or dew in the land. God took care of Elijah during the drought by telling him to camp out at a stream of water and by sending food parcels by raven delivery-service.

> Ravens are flying acrobats. They soar, twirl, roll and dive, especially if they are showing off to find a mate.

What's for dinner?

It definitely wasn't pizza! Let's hope Elijah wasn't a fussy eater because this takeaway service only had one option! The Bible says:

1 Kings chapter 17 verse 6

The ravens brought him bread and meat in the morning. They also brought him bread and meat in the evening. He drank water from the brook.

Common raven

Raven facts

These birds eat pretty much anything! They will snack on fruit, seeds, insects, small mammals or reptiles, eggs, garbage and even the remains of other dead animals they find.

Ravens are related to crows but are bigger and smarter. They have one of the biggest brains of any bird.

Ravens can be taught to mimic sounds, including simple words.

Bizarre behaviour

While it's true that ravens are highly intelligent, they are food scavengers who don't usually share outside their flock. Delivering food twice a day to a human is not normal behaviour for them! Why did they do it? The Bible tells us the answer: God said, "I have directed some ravens to supply you with food" (1 Kings 17 v 4).

God, who made the ravens and created their behaviour patterns, was the one who instructed them to carry out this life-saving food service. Even though living through a drought was hard for Elijah, God cared about him so much that he made birds known as "an unkindness" to become kind. What an amazing Rescuer!

What's that word: Prophet

A prophet is someone God chooses to be his messenger. Prophets delivered messages to people from God, often about something that would happen in the future.

LIONS ON A DIET

"Salad? Yuck!"

"I think I'd rather have a salad," said no lion EVER! It's true that lions are from the cat family, but they are not our furry friends. They are carnivores (meat eaters), eating up to a quarter of their body weight in a single meal.

Male lions hunt for food alone, while the smaller females are more tactical and work together to hunt down their prey. When lions are mentioned in the Bible it is usually because of their ferocious nature and their nasty habit of hurting people.

Here comes dinner!

The Bible tells an incredible story about some hungry lions. "Food" was delivered to them when a good man called Daniel was thrown into their den as punishment for praying to God. This was organised by some horrible, jealous rivals. The den was sealed shut with a big stone. And that's where Daniel spent the night. With the lions. In their den!

Lions don't live in dens in the wild—but in ancient times, they were sometimes captured and kept in enclosures by kings.

Historical backstory

This lion incident took place in the country of Babylon. The Babylonians had invaded Israel and conquered God's people, taking away the best and brightest young men (including Daniel) as captives. Daniel shone out as a smart, honest, hardworking, faithful person, and soon became an advisor to the king... and the next king... and the king after that! By the time we get to the story about being thrown to the lions, Daniel would have been at least 70 years old!

It's amazing!

Lions are predators—they usually eat people when they have the chance. But God is even more powerful than lions! He has angels who can stop lions from people-munching. Daniel trusted God to save him from this unfair punishment. And God did.

Roarsome facts

A group of lions is called a pride. No other big-cat species lives in groups.

African lion

African lioness

African lion cub

Lions are the only member of the big-cat family who roar in unison.

Approximately 100 people are killed by lions every year.

How did Daniel survive?

The Bible tells us how Daniel survived his encounter with the lions:

Daniel chapter 6 verses 19–22

[19] As soon as the sun began to rise, the king got up. He hurried to the lions' den. [20] When he got near it, he called out ... "Daniel! You serve the living God. You always serve him faithfully. So has he been able to save you from the lions?" [21] Daniel answered, "Your Majesty, may you live for ever! [22] My God sent his angel. And his angel shut the mouths of the lions. They haven't hurt me at all."

What's that word: Angel

The word angel means *messenger*. Angels are powerful heavenly beings that look like men and deliver messages for God.

HOW BIG WAS THAT FISH?

Giants of the Sea

Blue whales are the largest creatures on the planet, but whales are not fish. They are mammals, who give birth to live young and need air to breathe.

Blue whales can grow up to 30 metres (100 feet) long.

If you know any fishermen, you'll know they sometimes exaggerate the size of the fish they catch. But what if the enormous fish catches *you*?

What happened?

God asked Jonah to do a job for him. It was a tough job, and probably a bit scary. Jonah didn't want to go where God was sending him, so he ran away. He boarded a boat and tried to go as far in the opposite direction as he could. But of course, running away from the God of the universe is not that simple. God stirred up a storm and Jonah ended up overboard. The Bible says, "Now the LORD sent a huge fish to swallow Jonah. And Jonah was in the belly of the fish for three days and three nights" (Jonah 1 v 17).

30 metres

Blue whale

18 metres

Sperm whale

That's BIG!

16 metres

Humpback whale

The whale shark is a fish, not a whale. It's the biggest fish in the sea!

Where in the world?

Jonah was heading *west* (away from Israel) on the Mediterranean Sea when the boat struck trouble in the storm. God had told him to go *north-east* to the city of Nineveh.

What kind of fish?

The story of Jonah being swallowed by a gigantic fish is a whale of a tale... but the Bible doesn't tell us what kind of fish swallowed Jonah. It may have been a type of whale, a large fish, or perhaps even a sea creature that is now extinct.

Humpback whales have the longest flippers in the world.

Baby whales are called calves and are the biggest babies on the planet, at up to 8m (26 feet) long when born.

Sperm whales and blue whales win the noisiest-animal prize. Their calls are louder than jet engines and can be heard up to 1600 km (1,000 miles) away!

A blue whale's tongue can weigh as much as an elephant.

Humpback whale

African elephant

Sperm whales

Is it really true?

Did this *Jonah and the fish* story really happen? Could someone really get swallowed by a giant sea creature, survive in its belly for three days and then be spat out alive, as the Bible describes in the book of Jonah? Even if science could prove it was possible (although there probably won't be many volunteers for that experiment), don't forget the God factor. God can do more amazing things than we could even imagine—like creating the whole world!

Did you know that Jesus believed that this story about Jonah was true? Jesus compared himself dying and coming back to life with what happened to Jonah.

Jesus said, "Jonah was in the belly of a huge fish for three days and three nights. Something like that will happen to the Son of Man [Jesus]. He will spend three days and three nights in the grave" (Matthew 12 v 40).

THE SHEEP WHO FOUND OUT FIRST

Have you ever been out in the country and gazed at the stars? On a clear night you might even see a shooting star or a comet. On the night Jesus was born, some sheep and shepherds in a field outside Bethlehem saw something even more astonishing than that...

Luke chapter 2 verses 8-11

8 There were shepherds living out in the fields nearby. It was night, and they were taking care of their sheep. 9 An angel of the Lord appeared to them. And the glory of the Lord shone around them. They were terrified. 10 But the angel said to them, "Do not be afraid. I bring you good news. It will bring great joy for all the people. 11 Today in the town of David a Saviour has been born to you. He is the Messiah, the Lord."

Top of the list

Why were shepherds and sheep the first to hear the exciting news about God's Son, Jesus, being born? Shepherds were slightly smelly, ordinary people. Why didn't God tell important religious leaders first? Or powerful rulers and kings?

The angel said that Jesus being born was *good news for all people*. God sent his Son for everyone, no matter how important they seem, how young or old they are, or even if they smell like sheep!

A sheep's life in the Bible

Sheep are mentioned in the Bible more than any other animal.

Sheep were regularly used as a sacrifice to honour God (see pages 10-11, *Flocks and Herds*).

Shepherds often slept in the fields with their flock, to protect them from night predators. This also gave them that slightly smelly reputation.

A common breed in Israel was called the fat-tailed sheep. Can you guess why?

What's that baby's name?

Wasn't it *Jesus* who was born that night? How many names and titles does he have?

Quite a few! Jesus was his given name, but he is often known as the Saviour, Messiah or Christ. These titles point to Jesus fulfilling God's promise to send a Rescuer-King to save his people. When Jesus was an adult, he was also called "the Lamb of God" (John 1 v 29).

What's the big deal about sheep?

Why do sheep get so much attention in the Bible? And how is Jesus like a lamb?

God had set up special ways for his people to honour him, thank him, say sorry for their mistakes, and remember times when he rescued them (see pages 12-13, *Frog Overload*). This sometimes involved offering animals as a sacrifice, including sheep.

Jesus was born for a much bigger, more important rescue. He came to rescue us from sin, which wrecks our friendship with God.

When Jesus died, it was like a sacrifice—but then he came back to life, achieving the greatest rescue ever and restoring our friendship with God! That really is good news! Read all about the way Jesus rescued us on page 43.

LOCUSTS FOR LUNCH

What's your favourite snack? Is it something crunchy? Perhaps you have a sweet tooth? Or maybe you like healthy snacks? I wonder if anyone's favourite is crispy fried grasshopper...

Who eats grasshoppers?

Several cultures in the world eat insects as a special treat, including parts of Africa, the Middle East and Asia. Grasshoppers can be fried, smoked, dried or even cooked on a skewer. In the Bible, an interesting character called John the Baptist lived in a desert region and Mark 1 v 6 tells us he was known for eating locusts and wild honey. In Jewish law, locusts, crickets and grasshoppers are the only kind of insects that are allowed to be eaten.

The Judean wilderness, where John liv

Crazy cousin

Even though John's diet of locusts and honey was odd, that wasn't his main claim to fame. John and Jesus were related to each other.

Both had their birth unexpectedly foretold by an angel; both were given specific jobs by God; and they were only a few months apart in age.

John's birth fulfilled a prophecy from hundreds of years earlier in the Bible, that someone would come to prepare the way for the coming Rescuer-King: his cousin Jesus. John told people to repent—to turn away from a life of doing whatever they wanted and turn back to loving God.

Not-so-fun facts about locusts

Locusts are large, winged grasshoppers that live in most parts of the world.

Short-horned grasshopper

They usually live alone, until certain weather conditions trigger an unusual change in their behaviour. Then, locusts suddenly love being around each other! Their breeding multiplies, and they swarm together.

When locusts swarm, there can be billions of them munching, marching, flying and destroying every crop in their path.

Swarming only happens occasionally, not every year.

at green bush-cricket

Locusts can eat their body weight in plants every day. The sound of billions of locusts chewing can be heard from a great distance away.

Migratory locust

Florida lubber grasshopper

In the Bible, locust swarms or plagues are likened to an army moving through and destroying the land.

Field cricket

From a distance, a locust swarm looks like a big, black, moving cloud.

he River Jordan, where John baptised people

What's that word: Baptism

John was called "John the Baptist" because he was baptising people—dipping them under the water. It wasn't to clean their skin though. John encouraged people to be baptised as a symbol of being washed clean from sin (see page 9 to understand what sin is) and choosing a fresh start with God. Baptism is still a key part of church life today.

A VERY FISHY MIRACLE

Wherever Jesus went, unusual things happened. People were cured of life-long diseases, one boy's packed lunch fed an entire crowd of thousands, storms stopped when Jesus told them to. Wow! A *miracle* is something so amazing and unusual that only God could do it—and Jesus did plenty of miracles. On this day, a very fishy miracle was about to happen!

Luke chapter 5 verses 1 and 4-6

[1] One day Jesus was standing by the Sea of Galilee. The people crowded around him and listened to the word of God ... [4] When he finished speaking, he turned to Simon. Jesus said, "Go out into deep water. Let down the nets so you can catch some fish."

[5] Simon answered, "Master, we've worked hard all night and haven't caught anything. But because you say so, I will let down the nets." [6] When they had done so, they caught a large number of fish. There were so many that their nets began to break.

There are many species of fish in the Sea of Galilee, but there are three main species that fishermen try to catch and sell. One of them, the musht, is even nicknamed "St Peter's fish".

Tilapia or 'musht'

Trusting what Jesus says

When Jesus told Simon to try again—after fishing ALL NIGHT—I wonder what Simon felt and thought? Maybe he couldn't think properly at all because he was so tired and frustrated from his unsuccessful night. Check out Simon's attitude though. His response to Jesus was yes: "because you say so". Simon didn't trust his feelings or his thoughts—he trusted *Jesus*. That's what followers of Jesus do.

Fishy facts

All fish are cold-blooded like reptiles.

Fish don't have lungs like mammals but use their gills to breathe underwater.

Fishermen on the Sea of Galilee would often work at night so that the fish wouldn't see their nets in the water... which is why catching a huge amount of fish in the daytime really is miraculous.

Bohar snappers in the Red Sea

Beside the seaside?

The Sea of Galilee is an inland freshwater lake, not part of the ocean. Fishing has been an important part of life there for thousands of years, and still is. The town of Nazareth, where Jesus grew up, is near the Sea of Galilee. Jesus taught many crowds of people in this region about God's kingdom.

Many names

The Sea of Galilee is sometimes known by other names in the Bible, depending on which language the writer was using. It was originally known as the Sea of Kinneret, which it is also called in Israel today.

Simon is known by another name too. Jesus renamed him Peter (sometimes he is called Simon Peter), which means "rock". Simon Peter went on to become one of the founders of the Christian church, teaching people about everything Jesus had done and said. He became a fisherman of people for Jesus!

GOD LOOKS AFTER SPARROWS

Male

Sparrows are one of the most common birds on the planet, living on every continent except Antarctica. You've probably seen them: they are those small, grey-and-brown birds often sitting in a row on overhead powerlines. Or perhaps you've heard them chirping noisily together as they collect food. Sparrows were a common sight in Bible times too.

Male and female sparrows look different. Males have black cheek patches and bibs, and a darker 'cap' on their head. Females are lighter brown with a pale eye stripe.

Female

Sparrows in the spotlight

Jesus talked about sparrows while he was teaching people to trust God. He said:

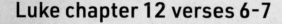

Luke chapter 12 verses 6-7

⁶ Aren't five sparrows sold for two pennies? But God does not forget even one of them. ⁷ In fact, he even counts every hair on your head! So don't be afraid. You are worth more than many sparrows.

Male house sparrows in the UK have a grey "cap" on top of their head. Tree sparrows (a less common variety) have a chestnut-brown cap.

House sparrow

Do the numbers

If God counts every hair on your head, and every hair on everybody else's heads... Wow that's a big number! But Jesus wasn't trying to highlight God's good counting ability. He was telling his listeners that God knows them. Check out Psalm 139 v 1-6 for confirmation that God loves you and knows you inside and out!

Sparrow chitchat

Sparrows forage for food, usually along the ground, but they aren't fussy eaters. They snack on seeds, grains, insects, or crumbs that humans leave behind.

House sparrows are a common variety. They prefer to nest in crevices in man-made structures, which doesn't make them popular with most homeowners!

Sparrows are flock birds—they hang out in groups.

CHATTER

CHIRP

Tree sparrow

CHIRP

Like many birds, sparrows mate for life. This means that sparrows will keep the same partner over their lifetime. But if one bird dies, the other will find another mate.

Cheeky, chirpy, busy and social, sparrows seem to like chattering all at the same time!

Historical side note

If sparrows were so common, what were people buying them for?

In the Bible, a small bird like a pigeon, dove or sparrow was acceptable for some sacrifices (see page 11 for more info on sacrifices and offerings). That's one reason why people would have bought them. It's also possible that people who couldn't afford much meat bought them at the market to cook for dinner, like a chicken drumstick or as a kebab.

Low cost but high value

In another part of the Bible (Matthew 10 v 29-31), Jesus says that two sparrows cost one penny, but Luke writes that you can get five sparrows for two pennies. These birds are so common and so unimportant that you could buy four, get one free! But God cares about them. He notices them. He doesn't forget them—not even the freebie. Jesus said that ordinary birds who aren't even worth a penny matter to God. And you matter much, much more.

REMEMBER TO FEED THE DOG!

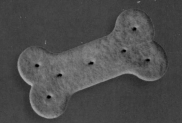

Whether big or small, playful or protective, workers or companions, dogs are the most popular pet on the planet. They are mentioned quite a few times in the Bible, but not as "man's best friend". In fact, our favourite pet has a rotten reputation in most of the Bible. What's that about?

Cocker Spaniel

Jack Russell Terrier

What did Jesus say?

Did you know that Jesus mentioned dogs? The conversation started when a woman begged Jesus to cure her daughter.

Border Terrier

Matthew chapter 15 verses 25-28

25 Then the woman fell to her knees in front of him. "Lord! Help me!" she said.

26 He replied, "It is not right to take the children's bread and throw it to the dogs."

27 "Yes it is, Lord," she said. "Even the dogs eat the crumbs that fall from their owner's table."

28 Then Jesus said to her, "Woman, you have great faith! You will be given what you are asking for." And her daughter was healed at that moment.

West Highland White Terrier

Burnese Mountain Dog

Looking deeper

Was Jesus being rude to this woman? No! So what do his words mean?

The woman, who was not Jewish, asked Jesus to cure her daughter.

Children stands for God's people, the Jews. *Bread* stands for the good things God gives his people, including Jesus' miracles of healing. The word for *dog* that Jesus uses here isn't an insult—it means a little dog, or pet.

Jesus was saying that his priority was to keep God's promises *to his people first*—just as parents would feed their children first, then give the pet dog the leftovers, not the other way around.

The woman agreed with Jesus, but she didn't give up! She knew that "crumbs" of Jesus' power would be better than nothing—and she was right!

A brief history of dogs

The first part of the Bible, the Old Testament, often refers to dogs as wild scavengers that roamed in packs scrounging for food. They were not welcome in towns or homes.

Creating new breeds of dogs became popular in the 1800s. Before then, there were nowhere near as many dog breeds as there are now.

Different parts of the world disagree on how many dog breeds there are, but it's between 195 and 400! How many do you know?

Dalmatian

Pug

Border Collie

German Shepherd

Australian Shepherd

Corgi

Dachshund

Modern domestic dogs are all descendants of wolves.

Israel's neighbouring countries were much fonder of dogs. Some even worshipped them.

P.S. These days, anyone and everyone can be part of God's family! See page 44 to find out how God used animals to tell people that everyone is welcome into his family.

What's that word: Testament

The Bible is divided in two parts: the Old Testament, at the beginning of the Bible, and then the New Testament. A *testament* tells facts or records an agreement.

IN THE PIGPEN

Have you ever had a really bad day? Jesus told a parable about a young man whose worst day ever made him wish he could eat pig food. That's pretty bad!

What's the story?

The parable Jesus told is about two sons and a father. The younger son rudely demanded his inheritance money before he deserved it. As soon as he had his share of the father's money, he travelled to another country and wasted it all. When food ran out in that land, the young man found himself with no money, no food and no friends. He had to take any job he could. So he ended up with the worst job a Jewish person could have: feeding pigs.

What happens in the end?

Eventually the son decided to go home and beg his father's forgiveness. He hoped that if he worked as a servant for his father, he would at least get fed:

Truffles are a pig's favourite food!

YUM!

Luke chapter 15 verse 20

While the son was still a long way off, his father saw him. He was filled with tender love for his son. He ran to him. He threw his arms around him and kissed him.

Read the whole story in Luke 15 v 11-32.

OINK!

This little piggy...
Pigs have poor eyesight, but an excellent sense of smell.

They use their strong, super-sensitive snout to forage for grubs and the roots of plants in the ground. Pigs can even be trained to sniff out fungi called truffles that grow underground.

?!

To "eat like a pig" means that you eat greedily—because pigs will eat pretty much anything, and quite a lot of it!

Some people think pigs are the smartest of all domesticated animals; even smarter than dogs.

Clean or dirty?

Pigs have a reputation for being dirty—but apart from **rolling in mud** to cool down, they are quite clean animals... unless you were Jewish. When God gave laws to his people about how they should live, he called some animals "unclean" to eat, including pigs. Apart from not chomping on a pork chop, Jewish people would not have wanted to hang around pigs at all!

The deeper meaning

Jesus told this parable to explain that God loves us like the father in the story. God never stops loving us. So if you're having a pigpen kind of day, whether it's because of your bad choices (like the younger son) or not, you can know that God sees you, and loves you, no matter what.

What's that word: Parable

A parable is a story with a deeper meaning. Jesus told parables about everyday things, such as farming, food and families, to teach people deeper truths about God.

THE OVERLOADED CAMEL

ave you ever packed your own bag to go away? How do you decide what to take? Even if you squash and shove as much as possible in your bag, one thing's for sure—you can't take everything with you.

Going somewhere?

Jesus once talked to a rich young man about going somewhere: to God's kingdom! Jesus used a big exaggeration to make a point. He said:

Matthew chapter 19 verse 24

It is hard for a camel to go through the eye of a needle. But it is even harder for someone who is rich to enter the kingdom of God.

Watch out for camel spit!

When camels feel threatened, they try to put their enemies off by spitting at them. But it's even worse than you think! It's a smelly mixture of saliva and vomit. Ugh!

YUCK!

What did he mean?

The kingdom of God is not so much a *place* as a *way to live*. It's believing in God's Son, Jesus, and living with God as your King.

Imagine a camel loaded up with rugs, clothes, spices, cookware and other goods. If a camel was going to fit through a tight, narrow opening like a small gate (not a real needle's eye), its owner would have to unload all those fancy extras so the camel could get through.

Jesus was saying that the rich young man's wealth didn't give him automatic entry into God's kingdom. In fact, there are no extras—not money, or a fancy house, or popularity—that make it easier for anyone to enter God's kingdom. It's only by *trusting in God's Son, Jesus.*

Camel capers

Camels often carry heavy loads, including goods and people, in remote places and harsh climates.

Arabian camels are found in hot, dry, desert environments, but the only place they currently live in the wild is Australia's outback! They were introduced there in the 1800s.

Camels are around 2 metres (6.5 feet) tall to the top of their hump.

There are two types of camel: The Arabian camel (Dromedary) has one hump. The Asian camel (Bactrian) has two humps. The camels in the Bible were probably Arabian camels.

Camels are nicknamed "ships of the desert" because they transport supplies across long distances.

This is a two-humped Bactrian camel. You can remember that because a 'B' has two humps!

Desert-dwellers

Camels are well-suited to living and working in the desert. They can go for days, weeks, or even months without water.

When they don't have a drink for a long time, their body uses the fat stored in their hump for energy.

Bible tip

If you read a verse from the Bible and you're not sure what it's about, try reading some verses before and after it. That can give you the bigger picture and help you understand its meaning. Read the longer version of this conversation starting from Matthew 19 v 16.

A KING ON A DONKEY

?!

If you were king or queen for a day, what animal would you ride to make your grand entrance? A strong, stomping stallion? An impressive, enormous elephant? Jesus chose a donkey.

Setting the scene

Jesus had been to Jerusalem before, but this was different. This time, people knew he had power to heal people's sicknesses, and they hoped he was the Rescuer-King God had been promising to send for many years. So why did Jesus arrive on a donkey? One of his friends, Matthew, tells us why:

Matthew chapter 21 verses 4-5

⁴ This took place so that what was spoken through the prophet would come true. It says ...

⁵ "See, your king comes to you.

He is gentle and riding on a donkey.

He is riding on a donkey's colt."

Not that kind of king...

In Bible times, a leader who rode a horse was on their way to *war*. A leader who rode a donkey came in *peace*.

God's people had hoped that the promised King would rescue them by leading a war against the Romans who ruled over them. God had a *much better* rescue plan that would bring lasting peace for all people! Jesus was the Rescuer-King God promised, but his rescue was not what people expected. (Read about that next on pages 42-43.)

The lowdown on donkeys
Donkeys have been used by people as work animals and transport for around 5,000 years.

Their large ears give them excellent hearing and they have very good eyesight.

Donkeys have a reputation for being stubborn. If they think a situation is dangerous, they will freeze and it's very difficult to change their mind!

Donkeys are slower than horses, but are very steady on their feet, even on rough or uneven ground.

Small donkey breeds are only 80cm (2.5 feet) high at the shoulder, while larger breeds can be up to 160 cm (5 feet).

Fulfilling a prophecy

When Jesus was on Earth, he fulfilled many prophecies that were made about him long before he was born. A *prophecy* is something that is predicted to happen in the future. God sent prophets (see page 21) to tell people what his plans were.

Royal celebrations

Luke 19 v 28-40 tells the whole story of Jesus coming to Jerusalem as King. He rode a donkey and people cheered him on, welcoming him, praising God, throwing down their cloaks to make a pathway and waving palm-tree branches.

In all of the loud celebrations, even though the donkey colt had never been ridden before, it calmly walked through a crowd of shouting people carrying Jesus, the King. Donkeys often dig their heels in and refuse to move when they are uncertain. Perhaps this donkey understood how important a King it carried.

WHEN A ROOSTER'S CROW MAKES YOU CRY

Have you ever heard a rooster crow? Their drawn-out squawk is loud enough to wake a whole neighbourhood at the first glimpse of dawn. But even though this is annoying, it doesn't usually make someone cry...

What went wrong?

Jesus had just arrived in Jerusalem to a king's welcome (see page 40), but not everybody welcomed Jesus as God's promised Rescuer-King. Some powerful people wanted Jesus dead.

Jesus knew there would be all sorts of sadness for him and his friends before his rescue mission was complete. He predicted that by the next morning, he would be betrayed and deserted by his friends—and then put to death.

The long night

Jesus was right. That night he was betrayed, arrested and taken away. Peter, one of Jesus' closest friends, tried to watch from a distance—he didn't want to get arrested as well! Three times, people suspected Peter was a friend of Jesus, and three times Peter said: "I don't know the man!"

COCK-A-DOO

Matthew chapter 26 verses 74-75

[74] Right away a rooster crowed. [75] Then Peter remembered what Jesus had said. "The rooster will crow," Jesus had told him. "Before it does, you will say three times that you don't know me."

Peter went outside. He broke down and cried.

It's no wonder Peter was upset. When Jesus needed a friend, Peter had let him down. But things were about to get much, much worse! When the rooster crowed, it announced the day that Jesus would die.

uOoOo

The most dominant rooster gets to announce the break of day first.

Polish chicken

Screechy facts
Roosters (male chickens) are bigger than hens, and are the boss of the chicken coop.

They have an inbuilt "clock" that tells them to crow at dawn.

Silkie chicken

Roosters may crow at any time of the day as a warning if they think their territory is under threat.

What kind of rescue is this?

Jesus came to rescue us from being separated from God. Back near the beginning of the Bible, Adam and Eve sinned (see pages 6-7) and it broke people's perfect friendship with God. Jesus came to fix that brokenness for ever! When he died, he took the punishment for our sin so our friendship with God could be restored. And if Jesus hadn't died, he wouldn't have been able to beat death by coming back to life. (Which is exactly what he did!)

The full story

Jesus dying and coming back to life is the most important part of God's plan to rescue people. Don't miss the full story in Matthew 27 v 32 – 28 v 10. (Spoiler alert: the first part is sad.)

I'm sorry!

How did Jesus respond when Peter let him down so badly? Jesus *forgave* Peter.

Peter's friendship with Jesus was restored and he spent the rest of his life telling people the good news about Jesus, because that really is something to crow about!

EVERYONE IS WELCOME

"You're welcome!"
"Come on over!"
"Would you like to join in?"
Isn't it nice when people make you feel welcome and included?

Once, God used a dream about all kinds of animals to do exactly that. He wanted all kinds of people—everyone, everywhere—to know that they are invited and welcome to be part of God's family.

The very strange dream

One day, several years after Jesus had died and come back to life (see page 43), Peter was praying while he was waiting for his lunch. While he prayed, he had a vision. Here's what happened:

Chameleons have prehensile tails, which means they can use them to grip onto branches just like a hand.

Panther chameleon

Acts chapter 10 verses 11-12

[11] He saw heaven open up. There he saw something that looked like a large sheet. It was being let down to earth by its four corners. [12] It had all kinds of four-footed animals in it. It also had reptiles and birds in it.

There are over 150 species of chameleons, ranging in size from 15 mm (1/2 inch) to 69 cm (2.25 feet).

Then a voice from heaven told Peter to choose something from these animals to eat (after all, it was lunch time!).

But to Peter, these animals were not allowed on the menu! No way would he eat those animals! Not even in a dream!

Crazy chameleons

Chameleons are amazing reptiles from the lizard family. Peter's dream included reptiles. Maybe there were chameleons along with the other animals.

Almost half of all chameleon species live on the African island of Madagascar.

Veiled chameleon

Panther chameleon

Chameleons have amazing eyes that can look in two directions at once!

They can change colour. Chameleons do this to warm up or cool down, to communicate how they are feeling, or to camouflage into their background.

... the story continues

What a strange dream! But even stranger than that, God sent Peter to see someone he didn't even know—a Roman Centurion called Cornelius—to explain what the dream meant.

Cornelius was not from God's family, the Jews, but he believed in God. Peter had been telling *Jewish people* about how Jesus loves and rescues us, but now Peter realised this message was for *everyone*!

Just like God included all kinds of animals, reptiles and birds in Peter's dream, God invites all kinds of people to be part of his family. People from different countries, different ages, different abilities: EVERYONE, EVERYWHERE is welcome! Anyone who chooses to believe in Jesus is welcome in God's family. (Read the full story in Acts chapters 10 and 11.)

You're welcome!

Sometimes we find it challenging to welcome and include people we don't know. It was a tricky change for Peter at first. But God is both welcoming and inclusive. Peter came to realise that "God treats everyone the same" (Acts 10 v 34). God really does love everyone, everywhere—including you.

What's that word: Vision

Vision is the ability to see. To "have a vision" is like seeing a dream when you're awake.

QUIZ TIME

This book has over 100 amazing facts about animals in the Bible. How many can you remember? Try this quiz to find out.

1 What colour was the dove that Noah released from the ark?

    a) White

    b) Multicoloured

    c) We don't know

2 Which of these is not a specific role in bee colonies?

    a) King bee

    b) Queen bee

    c) Worker bee

3 What was the most dangerous opponent David had to fight as a young man?

    a) A lion

    b) A bear

    c) A gigantic man called Goliath

4 What kind of birds did God instruct to deliver food to the prophet Elijah?

    a) Eagles

    b) Ravens

    c) Pigeons

5 God saved Daniel from being eaten by lions by...

    a) Providing the lions with other food

    b) Creating a secret exit for Daniel to escape

    c) Sending an angel who shut the lions' mouths

6 Which animals were there when the news about Jesus' birth was announced by angels?

    a) Donkeys

    b) Cows

    c) Sheep

7 Why did Jesus ride a donkey when he entered Jerusalem as King?

    a) Donkeys were his favourite animal

    b) To show he came for peace and not war

    c) To fulfil a prophecy

8 Peter had a vision about all kinds of animals. What did the vision mean?

    a) Peter was really hungry

    b) Peter should befriend all kinds of animals

    c) God welcomes all kinds of people to be part of his family

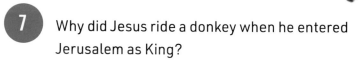

Answers at the bottom of page 2 (opposite the Contents page)

GLOSSARY

Archaeologist
A person who studies history by looking at what a past civilisation left behind.

Bethlehem
A small town in the south of Israel where both King David and Jesus were born.

Dominant
In some animal groups, there is a leader or animal in charge. The dominant male or female is often the biggest and strongest.

Eternal
Something that exists for ever and will never end—like God.

Gills
Part of a fish's body that enables them to breathe underwater. Fish have gills instead of lungs.

Habitat
The particular environment that is home to an animal species. An animal's habitat provides food, water, shelter and the right temperature for that species to survive.

Instinct
Animals behave or react in a certain way without thinking about it, depending on their instincts. Some animals naturally hunt for their food, while others have an instinct to hide from being eaten!

Israelites
God promised Abraham (see page 10) that his family would become a great nation and God's special people. Abraham's grandson Jacob was renamed "Israel" by God, and as time went on, Israel's family became known as Israelites.

Jesus
God's Son and the Messiah, who God promised would rescue people from their sin.

Messiah
God foretold through his prophets that a King would one day come who would save his people. The Messiah did come and his name is Jesus.

Metamorphosis
A process of changing shape that some animals go through in their life cycle. Frogs, beetles and butterflies all go through this process.

Miracle
An amazing occurrence that would not be possible unless God used his power to make it happen.

Pollen
A fine, powdery substance on or inside flowers.

Predator
An animal that hunts other animals to kill and eat them. The hunted animals are their prey.

Sacrifices and offerings
In the Bible, animals were sometimes killed and offered to God as a sacrifice to say thank you, sorry or to honour him. Animals were offered because they were valuable—it was like giving a gift to God.

Species
A species is a grouping of the same type of animal who can mate with each other to have offspring. For example, dogs are all one species, but there are several species of bears.

Territorial
When an animal guards or defends an area (a territory) they think belongs to them, they are being territorial.

Toxin
A poison produced by an animal.

Venomous
When an animal's poison is injected into a person or another animal by a bite or sting, that animal is venomous.

ALL ABOUT...

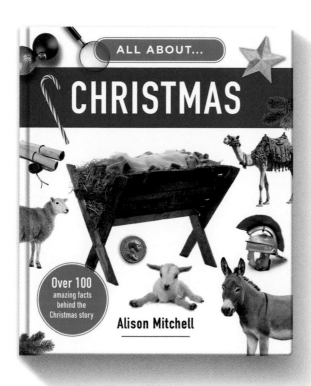

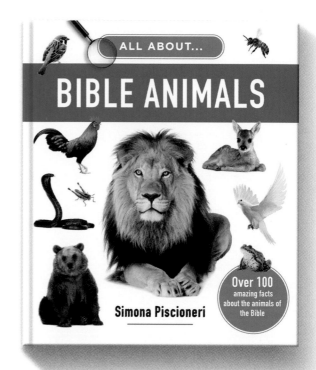

Unpack the amazing facts, characters and animals behind the events of the Bible. Dig into the history of well-known stories. Find out how God even uses animals to rescue his people. Explore maps and timelines that show where and when these true events happened. And discover why we can always trust God's word.

thegoodbook
COMPANY